5 Steps to a successful

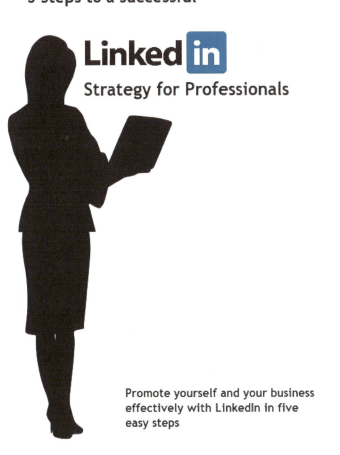

Linked in

Strategy for Professionals

Promote yourself and your business effectively with LinkedIn in five easy steps

5steps to a successful

LinkedIn Strategy for Professionals

By

Flambard Bolbeck

Edition 3 – 2012

fbolbeck@outlook.com

Table of Contents

LinkedIn for Professionals

Whilst the functionality of the LinkedIn website is relatively intuitive, many of the really useful functions are hidden away in menus. This author attempts to highlight the ways to optimise your LinkedIn presence and look at some real world applications that should be relevant to professional users and businesses.

This guide is designed for the busy professional who for some reason has yet to embrace social media. As little as two hours invested in maximising a LinkedIn presence can reap huge returns in new business and extended business networks.

Social media is the new normal for todays and more importantly tomorrow's clients to promote share and connect. Expectations are changing quickly and no LinkedIn presence or worse a poor LinkedIn presence may hold back your business.

Complete the **5**steps 'to do list' on the next page, sit back and watch a new world unfold.

5Steps **TO DO LIST**

When you have read through this guide tick the boxes as you build your online presence. When completed you will be ready to reap the benefits of the world's leading professional social network.

☐ **Create Your Profile**

☐ **Find Others and Get Connected**

☐ **Set Up Skills and Expertise**

☐ **Join Groups**

☐ **Participate in LinkedIn Answers**

1.   Why LinkedIn?

Brand Promotion

Attract new business

Collaborate with clients

LinkedIn is the world's largest professional network with over 80 million members and growing rapidly. LinkedIn connects you to your trusted contacts and helps you exchange knowledge, ideas, and opportunities with a broader network of professionals.

LinkedIn is a 'social networking' site that will prove to be of significant benefit to business executives and professionals in building contextual and collaborative networks. The phenomenon that is social networking can be dismissed or embraced but only ignored at your peril. There are many social networking tools and services, hundreds in fact but arguably the most popular business focused tool is LinkedIn. Essentially a networking site for professional people, it is rich in features some of which are ideally suited to professional services for marketing, business development, client collaboration, brand promotion and even sourcing new work.

This guide is not trying to be the definitive text book on LinkedIn and its multitude of features, instead we cover the key components we think will be useful to professionals such as company directors, accountants and lawyers.

Attracting proper public exposure helps potential clients find you.

2. Step 1- Create your LinkedIn Profile

Enables clients and prospects to connect with you.

Represents your career accomplishments and expertise.

Promotes your professional identity online.

Profiles come in two forms, People profiles and Company Profiles. Your personal profile when fully completed can be an extremely effective marketing and networking tool. It can display your specific areas of skill and expertise, prominent projects you have been involved with, education, work experience, etc. This helps prospects and clients searching for professionals with a specific background or expertise find you in search results.

Once you have connected clients, colleagues, peers etc. your LinkedIn network will reflect your professional relationships, promote your business, and maximise your likelihood of appearing in search results. In addition, LinkedIn profiles appear highly in Google search results, again increasing the chance of potential clients finding you.

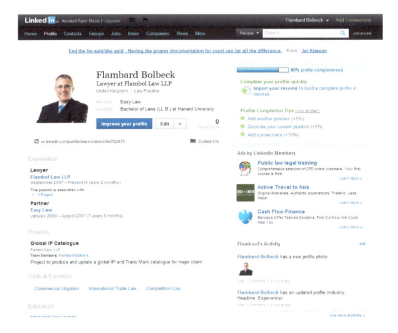

Quick tips for a Complete Profile

Photo

Whilst photos are not compulsory and many of us are not particularly photogenic (such as the author of this guide) the photo can be highly effective, especially with mobile applications on the iPhone or Blackberry. The ability to put a face to a name can be a very effective marketing tool, especially at conferences or gatherings.

Headline

This defaults to your job title but could be more informative. A headline is your 'first impression' chance to make a personal statement about who you are, or what your unique offering is.

Update

The 'post an update' feature allows you to publish a short statement about what you are doing or possibly a link to an interesting article you may have read (or written).

Experience

Your profile allows you to publish 3 recent positions held. Strategic use of this space will describe your key competencies and experience. A popular approach is to bullet point your 3 key responsibilities and 3 key achievements.

Executive Summary

A very important part of your profile as it allows others to find and connect with you based on key words searches. This area should be used to promote your specific expertise, career accomplishments and anything else that you wish to be known for.

Education

Where and what you studied provides an insight into your professional expertise, and may open up valuable connections to alumni or others with similar backgrounds.

Recommendations

When you write a recommendation for someone, you are expressly highlighting how that person added value for you. Recommendations received are a quick way for a potential client to see your expertise and strengths.

The best recommendations are brief and specific about what the person did and how they added value to your firm, matter or project and are a powerful way to raise the visibility of their skills and relationships.

Websites

You have the option to add 3 websites with either set categories like 'My Company' or 'My Blog' or you can create your own caption.

There are two key opportunities here, firstly these entries are indexed by Google therefore enhancing your firm's chance of being found, and secondly LinkedIn allows you to use a tag line to represent your URL (e.g. *The home of legal reference books* – a tag for www.amazon.com)

Add Sections

Some little used but potentially very useful areas can be added to the profile using the add sections feature. These areas are searchable and therefore help your clients or potential clients to find you when searching by expertise.

Languages

This enables you to add the languages you are competent in and the level of fluency you enjoy.

Publications

This enables you to promote any books or articles you have published.

Projects

A useful place to highlight key business or personal projects you have been involved with

Skills

This feature is particularly useful to summarise the key skills that are a subset of your main role. E.g. a Corporate Lawyer may wish to list M&A, Tax, etc.

3. Step 2 - Find others and get connected

> **See who you already know.**
>
> **Add connections.**
>
> **Let LinkedIn help you.**

At the heart of LinkedIn is the network of connections — the clients, colleagues and peers who acknowledge that they know you. To build a basic network you need to import existing connections from other 3rd party products such as Outlook or Facebook and then issue invitations.

Adding LinkedIn connections

Adding LinkedIn connections is very straightforward. There are a number of options of varying use depending on who you are trying to target. The 'Add Connections' option is currently at the top right of the screen alongside your name. This facility searches your existing contact database (in Hotmail or Gmail for example) and sets up invitations for you to send out.

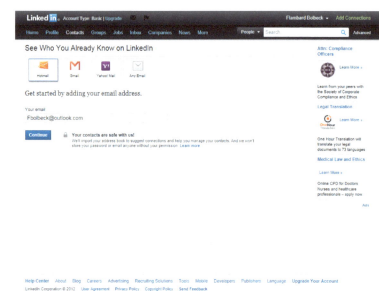

Search then add

You can search for a person, group or company by name in the "Search People" field at the top right of the screen. Useful if you know the name or company that you are trying to connect with.

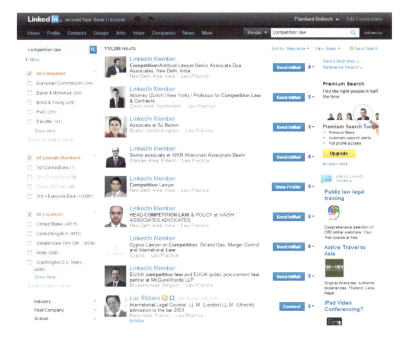

Your network

You can directly communicate with people who are your 1st degree connections, and you can see restricted information about people who are in your network's network or 2nd degree connection and even your network's network's network or 3rd degree connection.

When you want to communicate with a person connected to a 2nd or 3rd degree connection you must request an introduction from your 1st degree contact, who forwards your communication.

The LinkedIn Network

Outside of your 3rd degree network is the greater LinkedIn network, but you can only see title and company type unless you have an upgraded membership. As a 'Business', 'Business Plus' or 'Executive' member, you can send 'InMails' contacting people from the LinkedIn network to whom you are not connected.

4.   Step 3 - Setup Skills & Expertise

See an 'at a glance' holistic view of a particular expertise.

Ensure your profile's skills & expertise is optimised.

Endorse your peers and client's skills.

Slightly hidden away, the 'Skills & Expertise' page is under the 'More' menu tab at the top of the home page.

LinkedIn Skills & Expertise is a great place to discover the expertise that your peers, clients and other professionals have applied to their profiles and to see how the demand for these skills is changing over time. The statistical information shown is based on data LinkedIn members enter on their profiles.

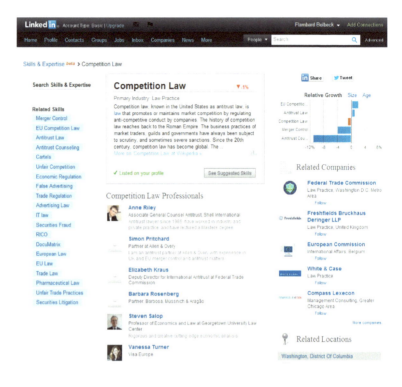

Visiting this section can also be a great prompt as to improving the skills section of your profile. A simple tweak from 'Competition Law' to 'EU Competition Law' could make all the difference to that next big client finding you.

Endorsements

A new and to some, controversial feature of LinkedIn in 2012 is the ability to endorse others skills & expertise. An endorsement is a one-click way for your connections to endorse the Skills & Expertise listed on your profile or indeed you on theirs.

To endorse a skill already listed on a connection's profile you simply go to the 'Skills & Expertise' section of their profile and click on the plus sign next to the name of the skill.

After you endorse someone, your name and picture will appear next to the skill on that person's profile and the person you've endorsed will receive an email. In addition an update about the endorsement will appear in both of your network update streams.

5.   Step 4 - Join Groups

Confine communication to selected users

Address hot topics

Keep information secure only to group members

LinkedIn groups are an excellent way to find and join like-minded communities of professionals. Once a member of a LinkedIn group you are able to view and participate in discussions, send group members direct and private messages and view jobs or announcements posted by other group members.

You can find the groups that may interest you by using the search function in the LinkedIn Groups Directory. Enter a keyword such as 'Competition Law' and any groups relating to that area will be displayed. Once you have applied to join a group you will either get an automatic acceptance or your application will be subject to review by the group owner.

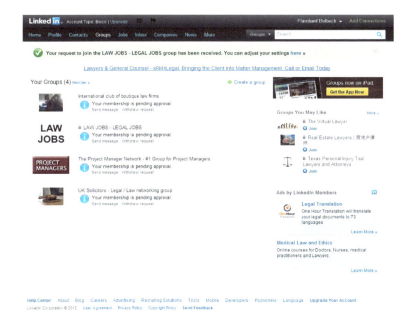

Four benefits of using LinkedIn Groups:

1 Create your own community

By starting your own group and inviting key clients and prospects to join you can develop a private community for topical discussions, knowledge sharing and general communication. It is also a great way to promote any events you are hosting or attending.

2 Contacting Group Members

Group members are able to communicate with each other without being connections. This is a great way to form new connections or clients without any formal introduction or invitation.

3 Member Polls

The built in and free 'Polls' feature enables you to do some quick market research and interact with other group members. Effective use of this feature, perhaps as a monthly poll helps generate continued interest in the group.

4 Job Postings

Separate from the jobs listed on the LinkedIn job board, the group based jobs are more likely to be relevant to the area of interest. Posting jobs is free and can be an extremely cost effective way to find that new recruit.

Setting up a Group - Best Practice

Always select a name for your group that clearly describes the purpose or brand.

Ensure the appropriate group type is chosen as it may impact how your group is found in searches.

Add an eye catching but appropriate logo.

State any group rules such as discussion guidelines, 'explicit selling' bans etc.

Encourage discussion participation and continuously update content.

Send out regular communications to all group members

Use the 'Poll' function to interact with the group members

Use the 'Mangers Choice' feature on a regular basis to promote the best discussions

Group Alert Emails

You may feel you get too many emails as it is but my own view is that the LinkedIn digest emails can be extremely useful. They are free and configurable by you so that you get the frequency of information that suits.

Available options are currently:

- An email for each new discussion
- A daily digest
- A weekly digest

My personal favourite is the daily digest which is a summary of any new information added to any of the group discussions an example of which is below.

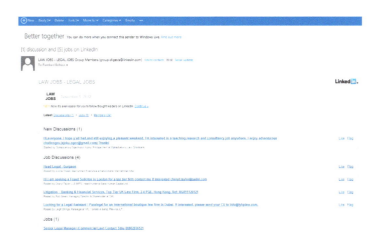

6.   Step 5 - Participate in LinkedIn Answers

> **Establish and maintain your personal brand by being a subject matter expert.**
>
> **Share (give and receive) free advice with a diverse professional network.**
>
> **Meet other professionals with the same interests and experiences.**
>
> **Discover potential networking contacts.**

LinkedIn Answers is a relatively new LinkedIn feature, which permits users to ask and answer questions to their network. The Answers feature is a great way to:

Promote your business - show prospective clients your expertise in a given subject area by answering questions and giving advice.

Connect with clients – use the Answers feature as a knowledge share amongst your clients and prospects alike. Clever use of this feature can be seen as a 'value add' to clients as well as a lead to new business.

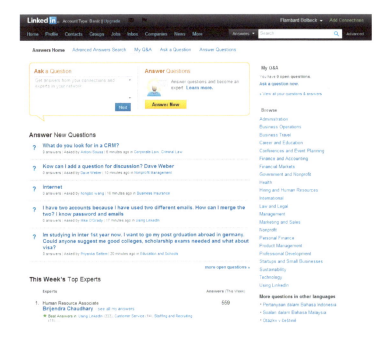

Asking Questions

Asking questions can be a quick (and free) way to get the information you need as well as a tactical way to seek out potential connections.

Your question may be answered publicly or privately.

Answering Questions

As well as demonstrating your expertise, a well-structured answer can be a great way to subtly market your business or self-promote as well as lead the reader to view your profile.

Answers Best Practice

- Keep questions simple and concise.

- Tactical questions should be of value to others.

- Avoid explicit selling, marketing and self-promotion. Subtle is king.

- Append text to questions where necessary.

- Don't leave a question open too long. When closing your question select the "best answer".

- Try and answer at least one question a month to sustain your brand promotion.

- The best answers are useful to the question originator but also require further communication.

- NEVER get involved in criticism or 'personal' exchanges.

Advanced features - LinkedIn Applications

Applications are a great (and free!) way to both enhance your personal or business profile as well as collaborate even further with any groups you administrate.

Applications are effectively 'add-ins' that appear on the bottom right of your profile and can not only provide you with great additional tools but also help you promote your business and share information.

Typically the Applications have a free install that gives you the basics with a n upgrade to some premium features. I have found the basics to be more than enough to add value to your LinkedIn presence.

An example could be a blog or news feed from your business website that appears on your profile generating greater exposure to your business updates.

New Applications are made available periodically so it is worth going back to this area of the LinkedIn site every few weeks to see if anything appeals.

Three of my favourite applications are as follows;

1 Wordpress

The Wordpress Application enables you to insert the latest blog or news feed from a specified Wordpress site. Wordpress sites can be elaborate websites or simple but effective blogs and can either be a great way to include headline information updates for your own benefit or to perhaps promote your company's site or blog.

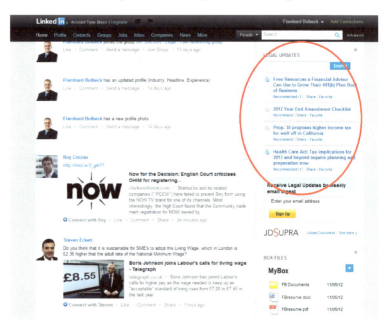

2 Box net

This is a great little application for saving and sharing documents. Most document types are supported making this an effective way to share or promote your company profile, Marketing Presentations, CV etc. Better still when a document is viewed or downloaded you will receive notification by email.

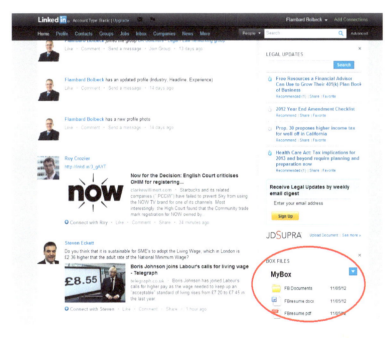

3 Events

With the LinkedIn Events app you can show your contacts which events you are attending or following. Additional features include;

- Personalized event recommendations based on your industry and connections
- Search tool to help find events in your location or industry.
- Attendees You May Want to Meet facility helping you expand your LinkedIn network.
- Download event to your diary feature.

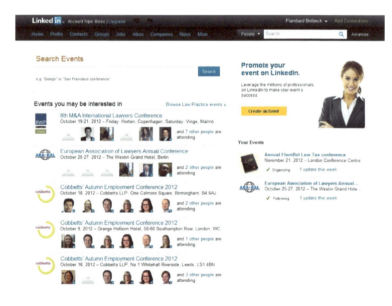

Promoting your own event

With LinkedIn Events you are also able to create your own event. Once created you can add all event details including; dates, summary description and logo.

The 'share this event' feature is a quick and free way to promote your event not only with your LinkedIn contacts but also within other social media such as Twitter and Facebook.

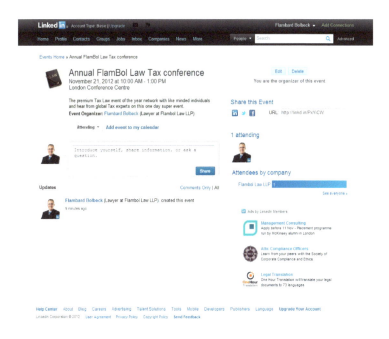

7. Using LinkedIn to maximum effect

Now that you've setup your LinkedIn account, like many things in life what you get out of it will be directly related to what you put in. Busy professionals simply don't have the time to spend updating an online profile all day although true rewards can be found if the quality of information you provide remains high.

Here are 3 maintenance plans to suit most diaries.

Presence Plan

This is the simplest way to maintain a presence on LinkedIn. Remembering a bad profile is much worse than no profile, a couple of hours effort can reap great rewards.

There will no doubt be people you have either worked or studied with with whom you've lost touch. In addition a good profile will help clients, head hunters, employees, event organisers and potential clients find you .

With a well formed profile, you enable opportunities to come to you.

Investment required – 1 to 3 hours

Network Plan

With a little more time investment, to expand on your profile you should develop a strong and focussed network. This is one of those areas where quality reigns over quantity so be selective over who you invite and who you accept invitations from.

Effective use of your LinkedIn connections can be akin to your very own private CRM system that updates itself as your connections move jobs, change details or progress their careers.

Two quick ways to activate your network are to import contacts from your Outlook address book, and to search LinkedIn for colleagues or contacts who are already members and invite them to connect. Once your basic network is activated, two effective ways to grow it are to keep an eye on who has 'viewed your profile' and who your existing contacts are communicating with on your 'Updates'

Investment required - 2 to 4 hours per week.

Expert Plan

This is using LinkedIn to the highest degree of involvement. The use of more advanced LinkedIn features such as 'Endorsements' 'Recommendations' 'Groups' and 'Answers' can help promote your own expertise and that of your firm and ultimately win new business.

Investment required -10 to 15 hours per week.

I hope you got some benefit from this guide. All comments welcome at fbolbeck@outlook.com

www.ingramcontent.com/pod-product-compliance
Lightning Source LLC
Chambersburg PA
CBHW041148050326
40689CB00001B/531